Show-Biz Quiz

Are you a keen film fan, a television addict, or interested in music, ballet, theatre or radio? And if so, how much do you know about your favourite entertainment? If you enjoy a challenge, try tackling some of the questions in this book. Some you'll probably find easy, while others will be harder, but all are great fun to do, and who knows, you may well learn more about your favourite stars and shows!

Robin May is well qualified to write a quiz on show business. He used to be an actor, and his great interests are the cinema, theatre, opera and the American West, on which he has written several books including another Beaver paperback, *True Adventures of the Wild West*.

SHOW-BIZ QUIZ

Robin May

Illustrated by John Adams

Beaver Books

First published in 1978 by
The Hamlyn Publishing Group Limited
London · New York · Sydney · Toronto
Astronaut House, Feltham, Middlesex, England

© Copyright Text Robin May 1978
© Copyright Illustrations
The Hamlyn Publishing Group Limited 1978
ISBN 0 600 383237

Printed in England by
Cox & Wyman Limited
London, Reading and Fakenham
Set in Monotype Ehrhardt

Front cover photographs by kind permission of Rex
Features (Clint Eastwood and Rudolf Nureyev);
British Broadcasting Corporation (The Goodies);
EMI Films Limited (Amanda Barrie in *Carry
on Cleo*); and Rocket Records (Elton John).

Contents

Introduction

There are more than 800 questions in this book, some of them simple, some hard, a few positively fiendish. All of them are about one branch or another of the entertainment industry – 'show-biz' as the Americans once christened it.

The subjects covered are films, theatre, television, radio, ballet and other forms of dancing, music, and song – opera, light opera and Gilbert and Sullivan. The pages have lots of different headings, but each subject may be recognised by the little drawing at the top of the page.

One or two points. . . . First, there are far more questions on films than on anything else. This is not simply because nearly everyone enjoys them, but because so many are shown on TV. In fact, nearly every Western, thriller, adventure film, musical, war film, drama and comedy that your parents and grandparents saw when they were young – certainly most of the good ones – have turned up on TV over the past five years, and they will turn up again. Thank goodness, many will say.

Secondly, in the music sections there are some, but not all that many, pop questions. This is simply because many pop numbers, even ones that get to the top of the charts, come and go rather fast, few of them becoming 'standards', which make for better questions.

And a final point about radio. You may wonder why the BBC dominates the questions so completely. The answer is simple. Our many local radio stations are just that – local and therefore not suitable subjects for questions. One London station has crept in, but only as part of a question about a famous actor.

And now . . . happy puzzling!

Let's go to the movies

1 Who sang 'Over the Rainbow' in which film?

2 If Robin Hood was a fox, what was Prince John?

3 What was the silent screen's comic police force called?

4 What sort of film do you associate with the composer Ennio Morricone?

5 Which of these was not a child star? Gregory Peck, Elizabeth Taylor, Mickey Rooney

6 What was Dumbo's problem?

7 Which Olympic swimmer became the most famous Tarzan of them all?

8 She was a princess in *The Swan* and then became one in real life. Can you name her?

9 For what type of picture is the director Alfred Hitchcock particularly famous?

10 Here are the most famous screen Sherlock Holmes and Doctor Watson. Can you name them?

11 Who are these two famous comics of the 1940s and
    '50s, and which is the fat one?

12 Name the all-star film about the Battle of Arnhem.

13 Its director also directed *Young Winston*. Can you
    name him and the actor who played Winston Churchill?

14 Which famous star of the *Carry On* films died in 1977?

15 Which screen dancer was partnered by Ginger Rogers,
    Rita Hayworth and Cyd Charisse?

16 What does the cameraman do in the making of a film?

17 What does a continuity girl do?

18 How many Disney Dalmatians were there?

19 Which child star became an ambassador?

20 Where is America's film capital Hollywood?

21 Which Saint was transformed into a Bond?

22 Who played the detective Hercule Poirot in *Murder on
    the Orient Express*?

Ring up the curtain

1 Sarah Bernhardt, the great French actress, played Hamlet. True or false?

2 Where are the lights actors call 'floats'?

3 Whose mother is Widow Twankey?

4 Who was France's greatest writer of comedies?

5 Canada has a world famous Shakespeare festival. Do you know where it is held?

6 Where did the National Theatre perform before its own theatre on London's South Bank opened?

7 If you 'fluff' a line on stage, what have you done?

8   Fill in the blanks to name these theatre knights:
    Sir Ralph —, Sir Alec —, Sir Michael —.

9   Where in Perthshire is there an annual festival?

10 The author of *The Deep Blue Sea*, *Cause Célèbre* and
    French Without Tears died in 1977. Name him.

11 In which pantomime does Buttons appear?

12 When did actresses first appear on the English stage,
    the 1560s, the 1660s, or the 1760s?

13 Which London theatre is the home of Variety?

14 Birmingham Rep is one of the most famous repertory
    theatres. But what is Rep?

15 Who was the most famous actor in Shakespeare's
    company?

16 Where in London is Shakespeare performed every
    year in the open air?

17 *The Importance of Being Earnest* is this Anglo-Irish
    playwright's masterpiece. Name him.

18 What is a 'comp' or complimentary ticket?

19 What is 'ham' acting?

20 Which is Ireland's most famous theatre?

21 Whom did Othello marry?

22 Who was the first actor to be knighted?

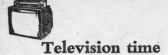

Television time

1   He played Sergeant Wilson in *Dad's Army*. Who did?

2   He was in charge at Fawlty Towers. Name him.

3   Which actress starred as Fleur in *The Forsyte Saga* and also starred in *The Pallisers*?

4   He is Hadleigh – and a disc jockey. Who is he?

5   Who is finally responsible for the pictures you see in a TV play?

6   Which actor linked *The New Avengers* with *The Avengers*?

7   James Bolam and Rodney Bewes starred in two hugely successful TV series. Can you name them?

8   Name these two actors who starred in a series.

9   When was the first BBC television transmission?

10   Who plays landlord Rigsby in what comedy series?

11   What is the name of Yorkshire Television's farm?

12   Who plays Corporal Marsh in *Get Some In!*?

13   Carmel McSharry starred in whose 'Lot'?

14   With which TV programme do you connect Frank Bough, Sue Lawley, Val Singleton and Bob Wellings?

15   What is the BBC's *Angels* about?

16   Which comedians have had Glenda Jackson, Vanessa Redgrave and André Previn as their guests?

17   Which actor and actress tried to find 'The Good Life' in Surbiton?

18   Who starred in *Callan*?

19   Who has a 'magic' way with animals?

20   Name the husband and wife especially associated with P. G. Wodehouse stories on TV.

21   Which two sports does Peter West cover for TV?

22   Which little known Dickens book was serialised brilliantly in 1977?

23   James Garner plays Rockford, but who plays his father?

Strike up the music

1 What was a troubadour?

2 What do brass players use to produce a much quieter sound?

3 Who wrote *Peter and the Wolf*?

4 Which famous pop group spells the second letter of its name backwards?

5 'Come into the garden . . . .' Who was the lady in the Victorian ballad?

6 Who wrote some very famous 'Water Music'?

7 What does 'forte' mean?

8 Which instrument sounds higher, a viola or a cello?

9 He started as a child prodigy pianist and became a great composer, a favourite with the ladies and an 'abbé' in holy orders. Who was he?

10 His *Clair de Lune* is one of the most loved of all piano pieces. Who is he?

11 How did Haydn's 'Clock' symphony get its name?

12 Louis Armstrong and Benny Goodman were great jazz trumpeters. True or false?

13 He wrote wonderful piano music but went mad and tried to drown himself. Who was he?

14 His *Flight of the Bumble Bee* has been performed on many different instruments. Name him.

15 Which soldier king played the flute?

16 Which instruments are played in a string quartet?

17 A Russian composer wrote a very popular fantasy overture, *Romeo and Juliet*. Can you name him?

18 Complete the names of these legendary band leaders: Glenn —, Duke —, Joe —.

19 Which is the odd work out? *The Christmas Oratorio*, the *St Matthew Passion*, *Israel in Egypt*

20 Which instrument does Yehudi Menuhin play?

Screen scene

1 This Man at the Top was in command at The Alamo, though he was British. Name the actor.

2 What sort of films did William S. Hart appear in?

3 What is an extra?

4 Which British actor played Nero in *Quo Vadis*?

5 What have these three historical characters got in common? General Gordon, Moses, Michelangelo

6 Who starred with Chitty Chitty Bang Bang?

7 Name the gap-toothed British actor who played the villain in *Those Magnificent Men in their Flying Machines*.

8 *Picnic at Hanging Rock* was a beautifully made mystery film. Where was it set?

9 Which famous Western lawman have Burt Lancaster, Will Geer and James Garner played?

10 Which queen of England have Bette Davis, Flora Robson and Glenda Jackson played?

11 What is Maurice Micklewhite's acting name?

12 Which is not a John Wayne film? *Hondo, The Man from Laramie, Fort Apache*

13 Can you name the first Beatles film?

14 In *To Catch a Thief* Cary Grant starred with which actress?

15 Who was married to Gary Cooper in *High Noon*?

16 Who was married to James Stewart in *The Glenn Miller Story*?

17 Who starred in both *Niagara* and *The Prince and the Showgirl*?

18 Who was the other star of *The Prince and the Showgirl*, and also the film's director?

19 Who played Zorba the Greek?

20 Which Hollywood star of the Thirties, Forties and Fifties was called 'The King'?

21 Which was Disney's first full-length cartoon?

22 Who are these three comedians?

On with the dance

1 Who invents the steps of a new ballet and rehearses the dancers?

2 Where is the home of the Bolshoi Ballet?

3 Who wrote the music for *Swan Lake*?

4 Which is the odd one out: Nijinsky, Melba, Pavlova?

5 Why is French the language of ballet?

6 What is a *pas de deux*?

7 Where is the principal home of the Royal Ballet?

8 When did dancers first dance on their 'points'?

9 She was born in 1919. Her name is Margaret Hookham and she grew up to be the greatest of all British ballerinas. What is her stage name?

10 Which is the outsider: *Così fan Tutte*, *Giselle*, *Les Sylphides*?

11 Alice Marks is better known as – who?

12 Who was famous for her dance, *The Dying Swan*?

13 What is a *pirouette*?

14 Who founded the Ballet Rambert?

15 What does 'elevation' mean in ballet?

16 How many basic positions of the feet are there in ballet?

17 With which country do you associate George Balanchine?

18 Name the hit musical which opened in London in 1976 and is about how dancers get jobs.

19 Ballet reached Russia in the nineteenth century. True or false?

20 When and where was the can-can first seen?

21 What is a *prima ballerina assoluta*?

22 What is the job of a *maître de ballet*?

23 When did the Sadler's Wells Ballet become The Royal Ballet?

24 Which is Italy's leading ballet theatre?

SCENE I
TAKE I

Spaghetti – and other dishes

Westerns made in Italy are usually called 'spaghetti'
Westerns, and, of course, some Westerns are made
elsewhere in Europe: Germany's are called 'sauerkraut'
Westerns! In fact, location work is often done in Spain,
parts of which look very like the American South-west.
Here are some questions on them.

1 Which was the film that made spaghetti Westerns
   world famous – and made a TV star a world star?

2 The director of this trail-blazing film was Sergio
   Leone, who followed it up with two sequels. Can you
   name them?

3 Kenneth More starred in a British comedy Western.
   What was it called?

4 *Custer of the West* was not shot in the West – but in
   which country?

5 And here are some titles for you to complete:

   a *A Professional* . . .

   b *Once Upon a Time in the* . . .

   c . . . *High*

   d *Navajo* . . .

   e *The* . . . *Gundown*

6 The two best known Commonwealth 'Westerns' both had Australian settings. See if you know their names:

a It starred Chips Rafferty and was about an Australian cattle drive.

b It was about an actual revolt by Australian gold miners in 1854.

7 And here's one for experts ....
It might be wrong to call *The Seven Samurai*, which is a Japanese masterpiece, a 'Western', but what famous American Western did it directly inspire?

8 Where was the British 'Western' *Diamond City* set?

On the box

1 What was the name of the *Blue Peter* dog that died in 1977?

2 One comic is called Little and the other —?

3 Who has 'short fat hairy legs'?

4 Which programme does Brian Moore introduce?

5 Who runs the Crossroads motel?

6 Who plays the Bionic Woman?

7 Who is in charge of the *South Bank Show*?

8 Whose ears were notable in *Star Trek*?

9 He is Harry O. Name him.

10 In which comedy show can you hope to meet all the leading politicians?

11 What do Michael Parkinson and Russell Harty have in common?

12 Who plays Fonzie in *Happy Days*?

13 Name the show in which the Muppets appeared before they got their own programme.

14 Who is the chairman of *Celebrity Squares*?

15 *University Challenge* has been popular for years. Who is the quiz master?

16 Who plays the Six Million Dollar Man?

17 How many of the *How* team can you name?

18 Adam West is Batman. Who is Robin?

19 Who plays Albert Tatlock in *Coronation Street*?

20 Which programme do you associate with Christopher Blake and Muriel Odunton?

21 Can you name the three Dimblebys well-known to viewers?

22 Dan Maskell talks about which sport on TV?

23 Who stepped from *The Main Chance* to *The Wilde Alliance*?

24 In *Two's Company*, Elaine Stritch plays Dorothy. Who plays her butler?

All the world's a stage

1 Finish the titles of these Shakespeare plays:
   Antony and —, *Timon of* —, *Troilus and* —.

2 Who wrote *The School for Scandal* and *The Rivals*?

3 Which Dickens book was turned into a hugely
   successful musical by Lionel Bart?

4 Old theatres had a 'green room'. What was it?

5 How many witches are there in *Macbeth*?

6 Who urges his men: 'Once more unto the breach,
   dear friends'?

7 Which musical begins with 'Oh, what a beautiful
   mornin' '?

8 What is Equity?

9 Greek actors wore masks. True or false?

10 An actor shot President Abraham Lincoln in a
   theatre. True or false?

11 He was born the same year as Shakespeare. He wrote
   Tamburlaine, the first great English play. He died in a
   tavern brawl. Name him.

12 How many Theatre Royal, Drury Lane, buildings
   have there been?

13 One of Scotland's best known theatres is in a poor
   area of Glasgow. Can you name it?

14 Russia's greatest playwright wrote *The Cherry Orchard*, *Uncle Vanya* and other classic plays. Can you name him?

15 What is New York's most famous theatre area called?

16 Who was the most famous playwright of the Chamberlain's Men?

17 Where did Captain Hook go to school?

18 Which bald-headed actor became a star because of his performance in *The King and I*?

19 Stage actors do their own make-up. True or false?

20 What is a 'dry'?

21 What does RADA stand for?

What's in a name?

These puzzle pictures represent the names of twelve well-known films. Do you know what they are?

Across the channels

1 *The Liver Birds* is set in which city?

2 Mr Hudson of *Upstairs, Downstairs* became a Professional. Who is the actor?

3 Who played the Mayor of Casterbridge?

4 The Coronation of 1937 was televised. True or false?

5 Who was employed to teach foreigners to Mind Your Language?

6 Name the Goodies.

7 Which actor commanded Dad's Army?

8   What was the name of Ronnie Barker's character in *Porridge* and what was the sequel to it called?

9   Val Singleton, before she joined the Nationwide team, was with a famous children's programme. Which one?

10 What is the name of the old music hall used in *The Good Old Days*, and where is it?

11 Cannon, Columbo, Ironside – which is the 'private eye'?

12 She played the piano in the radio show, *Have a Go!* and is now a *Coronation Street* star. Who is she?

13 Which world famous ballet dancer has appeared with the Muppets?

14 Which member of the Royal Family was the subject of an extra long *This Is Your Life*?

15 Who played Anna Karenina in the TV serial of Tolstoy's great novel?

16 Who is the outsider? Reginald Bosanquet, Kenneth Kendall, Angela Rippon

17 How did Lady Bellamy die in *Upstairs, Downstairs*?

18 He gave a sensational performance of the title-role in *I, Claudius*. Can you name him?

19 Can you name TV's Van der Valk?

20 Who is the question master of *Mastermind*?

21 TV's most popular poetess is . . . ?

Cinema story

1 Which is the odd film out? *True Grit*, *The Shootist*, *The Godfather*, *Shane*

2 Who was Liza Minelli's mother?

3 Who starred with Doris Day in *That Touch of Mink*?

4 Which is the odd animal out? Rin Tin Tin, King Kong, Lassie

5 Who was Popeye's girlfriend?

6 In which Disney film does Jiminy Cricket appear?

7 Which Hollywood studio do you associate with Bugs Bunny and Daffy Duck?

8 Who is the most important person in the making of a film?

9 Can you name these three famous comedians?

10 Which great clown of the silent screen and the talkies died in 1977?

11 Which screen Robin Hood also charged with the Light Brigade?

12 Which actor was 'swallowed' in Jaws?

13 Spot the outsider: *Carry On Sergeant*, *Carry On Constable*, *Carry On Up the Congo*

14 Who played the leads in *Butch Cassidy and the Sundance Kid*?

15 Which British knight starred in *Star Wars*?

16 For which of his roles did John Wayne win an Oscar?

17 Which is the wrong Road? *Road to Morocco*, *Road to Alaska*, *Road to Utopia*

18 Laurel and Hardy were both American. Right or wrong?

19 Which great actor starred in *Hamlet*, *Henry V* and *Richard III*?

20 How are Doris Kappelhoff, Marion Michael Morrison and Issur Danielovitch Demsky better known?

21 Which was the first James Bond film?

22 From *Bugsy Malone* to *Candleshoe* – which girl star made the move?

23 Which film-maker do you associate with the nature films *Beaver Valley* and *The Living Desert*?

News and views

1   He presents an afternoon *Newsround*. Who does?

2   Which newsreader is a *Face the Music* regular?

3   Once an actor, he now asks us to help the police in *Police Five*. Who is he?

4   A star for many years – and the shop steward in *The Rag Trade*. Who is she?

5   Who played Jesus of Nazareth?

6   Complete this sentence: 'Gemma Jones played the ... of Duke Street'.

7   Can you name Chris Kelly's popular film programme?

8   He may have half a finger missing, but this TV comedian is 100% when it comes to wit. Name him.

9   Brian Murphy is George, who is Mildred?

10   Where is Pebble Mill?

11   Who played Albert, the Prince Consort, in the series about Edward VII on ITV?

12   Can you name the series about the Royal Flying Corps?

13   Her legs caused a national sensation in a Morecambe and Wise show. Whose are the legs?

14   Which famous ship starred in *Sailor*?

15 Name these TV detectives (actor and part).

16 He was Marker, the Rev. Bronte, and Major Richter in *Enemy at the Door*. Can you name the actor?

17 Who made the very first television image of a moving object, and when?

18 In *Father, Dear Father* who was father?

19 When did colour TV begin in Britain?

20 Who 'invented' the Daleks?

21 What was the first sporting event televised in Britain and in what year did it happen: 1931, 1937 or 1946?

22 There was no TV in Britain during World War II. True or false?

On wings of song

1 The most famous opera singer of modern times died in 1977. She was a Greek–American. Can you name her?

2 Glasgow is the headquarters of which great opera company?

3 Bayreuth has a festival each year dedicated to which great composer (who settled there)?

4 Do you know when the very fine Welsh National Opera Company was formed?

5 Franz Lehár's masterpiece is an operetta called *The Merry —* ?

6 Figaro, the Barber of Seville, appears in the opera of that name and also in *The Marriage of Figaro*. Who wrote them?

7 Who is the outsider? Mozart, Wagner, Brahms

8 He lived in Suffolk at Aldeburgh, his first operatic masterpiece was *Peter Grimes*, and he also wrote for young people. Name him.

9 When was the Covent Garden Opera Company, now the Royal Opera, formed?

10 Which is the higher voice, mezzo soprano or soprano?

11 He composed *La Bohème*, *Madam Butterfly* and *Tosca*, three of the most popular of all operas. Name him.

12 Which Gilbert and Sullivan opera is set in Venice?

13 Who is considered the most important person in an opera performance?

14 Which famous opera features a hunchbacked jester and his beautiful daughter?

15 Who is the outsider? Caruso, Gigli, Gobbi

16 What is the name of Russia's most famous opera house and where is it?

17 Fill in the names: *The Magic —, Boris —, Billy —.*

18 Here is a scene from an opera loved by children and adults alike. Can you name it and its composer?

Movie time

1 Which author inspired a number of thrilling films including *20,000 Leagues Under the Sea*?

2 *Gold* is a short title. Who starred in the film?

3 In *Lawrence of Arabia* which Egyptian actor made a sensational first appearance in shimmering desert heat?

4 Who played the title role in *Oliver*?

5 Which twelve-year-old went about cheering everyone up in a Disney film and who played her?

6 Which veteran star played the doctor in *The Shootist*?

7 Who played the mother in *The Railway Children*?

8 Was Yul Brynner in *The Magnificent Seven Ride*?

9 In *My Friend Flicka* 'my' referred to a boy. What was Flicka?

10 George Lazenby played James Bond only once. In which film?

11 Everyone knows the Disney *Jungle Book*, but who played Mowgli in the 'live' 1942 version. Clue: he was Indian!

12 In which Disney film did a racing driver find that his car had a mind of its own?

13 He was America's most decorated war hero in World War II and, later, starred in many Westerns. Name him.

14 Who were the two British superstars in *The Man Who Would Be King*?

15 Who played the wizard in *The Wizard of Oz*?

16 Robert Shaw was stung in *The Sting*. Who stung him?

17 *Tell Them Willie Boy Is Here!* Willie was Robert Blake. Who tracked him down?

18 Richard Chamberlain and Gemma Craven starred in a Cinderella film. What was it called?

19 Which composer was featured in the Disney film, *The Waltz King*?

20 What was the name of the film about the Japanese attack on Pearl Harbour in 1941?

21 Here is Errol Flynn as General Custer. Can you name the film?

Keep in tune

1 Who was the composer of 'The Young Person's Guide to the Orchestra'?

2 How many symphonies did Beethoven write?

3 They play the drums, cymbals, triangle, etc. To which department of the orchestra do they belong?

4 In which work does the 'Hallelujah Chorus' appear?

5 Which big hit in 1978 do you associate with a Scottish promontory?

6 Who had a big hit with 'The Man from Laramie' in the 1950s and is now a famous disc jockey?

7 What is a concerto?

8 What does *pizzicato* mean?

9 Who is the outsider: Vivaldi, Rossini, de Falla, Scarlatti?

10 Who wrote the 'New World' symphony?

11 Which violinist was so brilliant that some said he was in league with the devil?

12 Whose symphony is 'Pathetic'?

13 Early in 1978 Cliff Richard sang with his old group for the first time in many years. Name it.

14 Who is the patron saint of music?

15 Here are three British composers for you to name.

16 Which Yorkshireman wrote 'On Hearing the First Cuckoo in Spring' and died in France?

17 Who composed the 'Unfinished Symphony'?

18 He was Austrian but he wrote a 'London' and an 'Oxford' symphony. Name him.

19 Who wrote 'Swanee River' and 'Jeannie with the Light Brown Hair'?

20 Which instrument did Adolphe Sax invent?

21 Who pictured his friends in 'Enigma Variations'?

22 Which great pianist became Prime Minister of Poland?

23 Who wrote a 'Fantastic' symphony?

Stage struck

Here are three famous actors (1, 2, 3) and below them –
which great new theatre (4)? Who is the playwright (6),
and what are these two very different types of theatre
(5, 7)?

Mickey Mouse & Co.

1   What part did Mickey Mouse play in *Fantasia*?

2   Which English actress played the title role in the epic film, *Gone With The Wind*?

3   Can you name the very first *Carry On* film?

4   Name the outsider: MGM, Paramount, Pinewood.

5   Who played Young Frankenstein?

6   How many nephews has Donald Duck?

7   Which British comedy had as its title the name of a vintage car?

8   Whose first film hit was *Love Me Tender*?

9   In which hilarious film series did Sir Lancelot Spratt appear and who played him?

10   Which American superstar was once a circus acrobat?

11   MGM studios made a long series of cartoons about a cat and a mouse. What were their names?

12   He played Hans Christian Andersen in a musical film. Who did?

13   'The Godfather' was also in *On The Waterfront* and *Mutiny on the Bounty*. Who is the actor?

14   How many Stooges were there in a famous old series of short comedies?

15 They enjoyed *A Night at the Opera* and *A Day at the Races*. Who did?

16 What was *The Longest Day* about?

17 She was married to Humphrey Bogart and starred opposite John Wayne in *The Shootist*. Who is she?

18 In which Disney film were you advised in a song not to smile at a crocodile?

19 Poor Sylvester never manages to devour – who?

20 When was Mickey Mouse born?

21 What is an Oscar?

22 Here are Doctor Dolittle and friends. Can you name the actor playing the doctor?

Turn on the radio

1 Who is the interviewer on *Desert Island Discs*?

2 When did the BBC begin broadcasting?

3 The most famous radio-comedy show of World War II starred Tommy Handley. Can you name it?

4 He chairs radio and TV quizzes including *Brain of Britain*. Name him.

5 What do you expect to hear Arthur Negus talking about on radio (or TV)?

6 Which sport does John Arlott describe on radio?

7 Who is the chairman of *Any Questions*?

8 Who starred in the legendary *Goon Show*?

9 Can you guess when the first BBC sports broadcast was?

10 A great Welsh play was first heard on radio. Can you name it and its author?

11 Who presents *Junior Choice*?

12 Edward Cast, Basil Moss and Ann Morrish are just three of the cast of which radio serial?

13 When did *The Archers* start?

14 What is *Kaleidoscope* about?

15 Who is the chairman of *Just a Minute*?

16 Whose *Letter from America* has been a popular feature every week for many years?

17 Who starred with Tony Hancock in the legendary series, *Hancock's Half Hour*?

18 Which BBC orchestra is world famous?

19 Who runs an 'Open House'?

20 What is *Any Answers* in answer to?

21 Who introduces *Country Club*?

22 Name these three disc jockeys.

Keep on your toes

1 Who wrote the music of *Romeo and Juliet* and *Cinderella*?

2 What is the corps de ballet?

3 Where is the home of the *csardas*?

4 Which nation's dancers use castanets?

5 What nationality is the dancer and choreographer, Katherine Dunham?

6 In which theatre did the Sadler's Wells Ballet perform before moving to Covent Garden?

7 In which ballet does the evil Rothbart appear?

8 With which theatre do you associate Maya Plissetskaya?

9 Copenhagen is the home of one of the oldest and finest ballet companies. Name it.

10 Who wrote the music for *The Firebird* and *The Rite of Spring*?

11 Whose ballet, *Song of the Earth*, is considered his masterpiece?

12 Fokine was a supreme figure in ballet history. What did he do?

13 Which German city did John Cranko turn into a centre of ballet?

14 Can you recognise this ballet?

15 What is the great double-role in *Swan Lake*?

16 Where might you see flamenco dancing?

17 Which ballet knights were famous Ugly Sisters in *Cinderella*?

18 What great French choreographer founded the Ballet of the Twentieth Century, based in Brussels?

19 Anthony — is one of Britain's finest dancers.

20 Which famous Sadler's Wells ballerina became Director of the Festival Ballet?

More movies

1 He played eight roles in *Kind Hearts and Coronets*.
   Name the actor.

2 Julie Andrews starred in the stage version of *My Fair Lady*. Who starred in the film?

3 Morecambe and Wise have made films. Yes or no?

4 Who was The Outlaw Josey Wales?

5 Name the tough Welsh actor who starred in *Zulu*.

6 He not only played Davy Crockett in *The Alamo* but also directed the film. Who did?

7 Pictured below is a comedian who often played schoolmasters. Who is he?

8 Warren Beatty played Clyde, who played Bonnie?

9 It starred Steve McQueen and had an amazing car chase sequence. What was it called?

10 What was *Born Free* about?

11 Can you name the actor who does the voices of Bugs Bunny, Sylvester, Daffy Duck and many other cartoon characters?

12 Who played Calamity Jane in the musical of that name?

13 Which famous comedian was born in Walworth, London, in 1889?

14 Who played Agatha Christie's elderly detective, Miss Marple, in films?

15 Bernard Schwarz starred in *Some Like It Hot*, *The Vikings*, *Monte Carlo or Bust* etc. What is his screen name?

16 What was the name of the very first 'talkie'?

17 Who played Long John Silver in Disney's *Treasure Island*?

18 Which film company has a growling lion as its trademark?

19 Which Australian actor received an Oscar after he was dead, for his performance in which film?

20 Who was called 'The World's Sweetheart'?

21 In which film did Gene Kelly dance in a downpour?

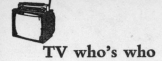

TV who's who

1 Who played the grown-up Edward VII in the TV series?

2 Ian Lavender played which gormless part in *Dad's Army*?

3 Name the series which made John Inman a star.

4 Who is the BBC's 'star' man?

5 Terry — and June — star in *Happy Ever After*.

6 Who starred in *Disraeli*?

7 He went from *A Man about the House* into a *Robin's Nest*. Who is he?

8 In which country is *The Magic Roundabout* made?

9 Who was the very first Doctor Who?

10 Which American film star played the lead in *Jennie*, the story of Lady Randolph Churchill, mother of Sir Winston?

11 'Sergeant Watt' made him a TV star. Can you name him?

12 Who invites viewers to 'Face the Music'?

13 Which ex-Doctor Who runs *Whodunnit*?

14 When did ITV start transmitting programmes?

15 Which is the 'dirty mackintosh' TV detective?

16 Who played Scottish schoolmistress Jean Brodie in the TV series?

17 Who was Godber?

18 Which 'good old' show does Leonard Sachs present?

19 Who sprang to fame as the awful Violet Elizabeth Bott?

20 Which series do you connect with Honor Blackman, Diana Rigg and Joanna Lumley?

21 Peter G — has been with which children's show for many years?

22 Name ITN's answer to Angela Rippon.

23 John —, Peter — and Lesley — presented which long running twice-weekly programme until recently?

24 Who played a famous Ancient British warrior queen?

Film festival

1 In which Charlie Chaplin film was he reduced to cooking his shoes?

2 Some say she is the greatest actress in screen history. She is Swedish. Can you name her?

3 Robert Donat played the schoolmaster in *Goodbye, Mr Chips*. Who played the part in the musical version?

In which film did George C. Scott play a tough, pistol-packing US general of World War II?

5 In *West Side Story – Romeo and Juliet* updated and set in a tough part of New York – Richard Beymer played the hero. Who played the heroine?

6 *Samson and Delilah*, directed by Cecil B. de Mille, came out in 1950, but is now more often seen on TV. Here are the stars. Can you name them?

7 Here he is, the most famous monster of them all, from the moment he played Frankenstein's monster in 1931. Name him.

8 Who played Captain Scott in *Scott of the Antarctic*?

9 What is a 'biopic'?

10 In which film did Burt Lancaster play an Apache?

11 Which superstar acted with Lassie and in *National Velvet* when she was young?

12 Who starred in *Little Big Man*?

13 Who was tortured by apes in *Planet of the Apes*?

14 It made a fortune and starred Julie Andrews and Christopher Plummer. What was it called?

15 The most famous film about World War II at sea starred Jack Hawkins as Captain Ericson. Can you name it?

16 This film was set in British India and starred Kenneth More, Lauren Bacall and a train! What was it called?

17 Who played Phileas Fogg and his servant Passepartout in *Around the World in Eighty Days*?

18 Father is Henry, son is Peter, daughter is Jane. Which famous family are they?

53

The play's the thing

1 George Bernard Shaw's most popular play is about a saint. Can you name her?

2 What is the name of the theatre at London's Puddle Dock, founded and run by Sir Bernard Miles?

3 A Scottish star of *Dad's Army* played Hamlet at the Old Vic Theatre in the 1920s. Name him.

4 Can you guess how many shows were on tour in Britain every week around 1900 – 75, 150 or 300?

5 What is an understudy?

6 What is a 'drag' act?

7 When an actor is resting, what is he doing?

8 A famous Welsh actor has given many Dickens recitals. Can you name him?

9 When was the first permanent English theatre built, in 1535, 1576 or 1588?

10 Who was the original Professor Higgins in *My Fair Lady*?

11 What is mime?

12 Where in Sussex is there a famous annual theatre festival?

13 What is the 'rake' on a stage?

14 Can you guess what a wardrobe mistress does?

15 Name the author of *Private Lives* and *Blithe Spirit*. He also acted, wrote music and lyrics.

16 Where is Shakespeare buried?

17 In which pantomime does Dandini appear?

18 Shakespeare wrote *Henry V*, *VI* and *VII*. True or false?

19 Who plotted the downfall of Othello?

20 Who is the father of Vanessa and Lynn Redgrave?

21 Which character in *A Midsummer Night's Dream* is given an ass's head?

22 Marlon Brando has appeared on the stage. True or false?

At the pictures

1 Lee Marvin's hilariously drunken gunfighter won him an Oscar in which film?

2 Who starred in *Tiger Bay*, aged twelve, opposite her famous father?

3 He was 'the spy who came in from the cold' in the film of that name. Who was the actor?

4 He first played the secret agent, Harry Palmer, in *The Ipcress File*. Name him.

5 Who was known as 'The Man of a Thousand Faces' because of his huge range of parts, many of them monsters!

6 Who played the title role in *Gigi*?

7 Which Disney film featured Sean Connery before he became James Bond?

8 What famous character did Lex Barker and Larry 'Buster' Crabbe both play?

9 In which film did Bing Crosby and Barry Fitzgerald both play priests and both win Oscars?

10 Father was a silent Robin Hood, son a star of the 'talkies'. The name's the same. What is it?

11 Her mother was Maureen O'Sullivan, Jane to Johnny Weismuller's Tarzan. Her films include *The Great Gatsby*. Name her.

12 Joan — and Olivia de — are sisters. Fill in the blanks.

13 Who was the American flyer in *Those Magnificent Men in their Flying Machines*?

14 And who was the English flyer?

15 In which film did Richard Todd play the famous bomber pilot, Guy Gibson?

16 Who played the lead in *Funny Girl*?

17 Which still popular singer showed he had tremendous acting talent as Maggio in *From Here to Eternity* and never looked back?

18 Why were Roy Rogers and Gene Autry unusual?

Take the right steps

1 Which great French artist painted many ballet dancers?

2 Which ballet was so revolutionary that it caused a riot at its Paris première in 1913?

3 Who was the founder of the Royal Ballet?

4 Name the electrifying Bolshoi ballet about a Roman gladiator who led a slave revolt.

5 Who became the queen of ballet in the Romantic era – the 1830s and 40s?

6 Can you identify this ballet?

7 Who caused a sensation when he brought Russian ballet to Western Europe early in the century?

8 Lynn — is a major ballet star who comes from Canada.

9 Who is Australia's ballet knight?

10 In which ballet does Doctor Coppelius appear?

11 Which famous dancer from the Kirov in Leningrad later partnered Margot Fonteyn with the Royal Ballet?

12 *The Red Shoes* is the most popular of all ballet films. Which Sadler's Wells dancer starred in it?

13 Some say he was the greatest male dancer of all. He was Russian, but died in London in 1950. He seemed to pause at the top of leaps! Name him.

14 Who is the Director of the Royal Ballet?

15 In which ballet does the Lilac Fairy dance?

16 In which opera do the sensational 'Polovtsian Dances' occur?

17 In which ballet does the Sugar Plum Fairy dance?

18 Some say it was the first really American ballet. Aaron Copland wrote the music and the hero is a famous Wild Western outlaw. Name it.

19 Sir Frederick — is regarded as the greatest of all British choreographers.

20 What is 'ballon'?

In the picture

Try these TV teasers. Hidden away in these pictures are the names of twelve television programmes for you to work out.

The magic of the movies

1 Rhett Butler was Clark Gable's most famous role. Can you name the film?

2 'I was born in a trunk' she sang in *A Star is Born*. Who was she?

3 This policewoman in the St Trinian's films never quite got her (police)man. Who was she?

4 Who was the Blonde Bombshell?

5 Here are three famous 'character men' for you to name.

6 Spencer Tracy was the Father of the Bride in the film of that name. Who was the bride?

7 William Holden led which bunch of outlaws in which film?

8 One of the most famous of all British stars was killed when his plane was shot down in 1943. Who was he?

9 Whose most famous role was as Jesus Christ in *King of Kings*?

10 Not content with being A Man Called Horse, he made a Return. Who did?

11 Which children's classic did the bald-headed actor Lionel Jeffries make into a film starring Dinah Sheridan, William Mervyn and Jenny Agutter?

12 He was Shane. Who was?

13 Who played the Cowardly Lion in *The Wizard of Oz*?

14 In *Becket*, Peter O'Toole played King Henry II. Who played the title-role?

15 Christopher Plummer played Wellington, Rod Steiger played Napoleon. What was the film?

16 Who displayed some sensational swordmanship in *Far from the Madding Crowd*?

17 'Wet she was a star.' Whom does that rather rude remark describe?

18 In which film did Rock Hudson and Elizabeth Taylor star with James Dean?

It's instrumental

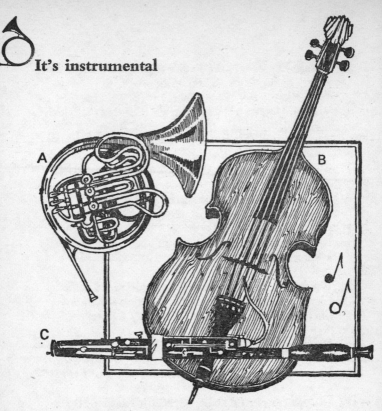

1 Can you recognise these instruments?

2 Who wrote *The Messiah*?

3 Who is the outsider: Elgar, Ravel, Vaughan Williams?

4 Where are the Proms held?

5 To which family of instruments does the oboe belong?

6 Which Scottish conductor is a knight?

7 Beethoven went blind. True or false?

8 He wrote the 'Moonlight Sonata'. Who was he?

9 Which Finn wrote seven symphonies and *Finlandia*?

10 Which is the outsider: Julian Bream, John Williams, André Previn?

11 How many strings has an orchestral harp?

12 Where is America's Country Music capital?

13 Which is a group of six musicians: quintet, sextet or octet?

14 Who wrote *The Creation*?

15 Chopin only wrote for the piano. True or false?

16 What sort of music do The Spinners and The Dubliners usually sing?

17 It was a 1978 hit by the Brotherhood of Man, not an opera by Mozart. What was it?

18 He wrote *Fingal's Cave* and gave Queen Victoria lessons. Who was he?

19 Which instrument does James Galway play?

20 How many strings has a guitar?

21 Which pop star 'stole' the name of a classical composer?

22 John Philip Sousa is best known for his waltzes. True or false?

23 Who wrote 'Rule Britannia'?

What a carry on !

1   Which of the ever popular *Carry On* films was
    a set in Ancient Egypt   **b** about the police
    c set in India   **d** about taxis
    e about the Foreign Legion   **f** about a school
    g about the army   **h** a funny horror film ?

2   There have been a number of regular actors and
    actresses in the films. Here are the first names of
    some of them, can you supply their surnames?
    a Kenneth W—   **b** Kenneth C —
    c Hattie —   **d** Sid —
    e Charles —   **f** Bernard —
    g Peter —   **h** Joan —
    i Jim —   **j** Jack —

3   And here are some questions for the real experts on
    the subject.
    a Who has directed all the *Carry On* films?
    b Who has produced all of them?
    c Whose inventive mind has managed to think up the
       gags for nearly all of them?

Time for heroes

1 Who played Carrington VC and was court-martialled?

2 The girl below played Violet Szabo, a World War II heroine, in *Carve Her Name With Pride*. Name her.

3 Another heroine of the same war was Odette, who spied for the French resistance and was tortured but, unlike Violet, survived. Who played her in the film *Odette*?

4 Lord Mountbatten's exploits in command of HMS *Kelly* and the deeds of his men were used by Noel Coward to make which classic war film?

5 Which popular star lost favour in Britain because *Objective Burma* managed to make no mention of the British Army's leading role in the campaign?

Turn on the telly

1 Even those who know little of Rugby League should know this colourful commentator's name.

2 Who introduces the BBC's *Match of the Day*?

3 Who plays Big John Cannon in *The High Chaparral*?

4 How do you connect Sarah Lawson with a prison?

5 Which weekend programme do you associate with Brian Walden?

6 Jim Henson is the mastermind behind which hit show?

7 Who play Nellie and Eli Pledge?

8 Which programme features Jenny Hanley and Mick Robertson?

9 Who plays the colonel of the unlikely bunch of soldiers in *It Ain't Half Hot Mum*?

10 The brilliant team who made *Sailor* later made a series about a British Crown Colony. Can you name it?

11 Name 1978's Lorna Doone.

12 What type of programme does Robert Erskine present?

13 With which sport do you connect Peter O'Sullevan?

14 Which British actor starred in the final episodes of *The Virginian*?

15 His brother is a famous actor-director and he presents natural history and travel programmes on television. Name him.

16 Who are these three top TV comics?

17 Who is television's James Herriot in *All Creatures Great and Small*?

18 William — smoothly and wittily stars in *What's On Next*?

19 Who plays Jack Lord's colleague in *Hawaii Five-O*?

20 Name the actor married to the snobbish Margo in *The Good Life*.

21 Who says to each victim: 'This is your life!'?

22 Which family live in the 'Little House on the Prairie'?

Camera angles

1 A coach finds a young Tarzan in Africa. Can you name the Disney film?

2 They tunnelled under a vaulting horse to escape from a German prisoner-of-war camp. Name the film.

3 Four children in the Lake District and their adventures – name the 1974 film about them.

4 In which Disney film did John Mills play the father of a shipwrecked family?

5   It became a TV favourite, but who starred in the original film of M*A*S*H?

6   Chief Dan George made a great impression in a film starring Dustin Hoffman. Can you name it?

7   The couple opposite sang together in romantic films of the 1930s like *Rose Marie* and *The Girl of the Golden West*. Can you name them?

8   Name the Yorkshire-born actor who starred as Henry VIII, King Herod and the Hunchback of Notre Dame.

9   In which musical did Julie Andrews have a wild time in the 1920s?

10 *Airport* starred Burt Lancaster. Who starred in *Airport* 75?

11 In which Disney film is Thumper the Rabbit one of the stars?

12 Who had a long long fight in *The Big Country*?

13 Charles Bronson likes his wife to be in his films. Can you name her?

14 Who played Sherlock Holmes' smarter Brother?

15 Flubber enabled him to drive his car through the sky. The actor was Fred MacMurray, what was the film?

16 In *The Quiet Man* John Wayne had a very long fight with which actor?

17 Which of these is not a James Stewart film: *The Far Country*, *The Naked Spur*, *Johnny Concho*?

The baddies

Here are questions entirely devoted to the bad guys, who so cheer us all up!

1 In *Mutiny on the Bounty* he was Captain Bligh, in *Jamaica Inn* he was a shipwrecker. Name him.

2 At least he was a funny villain in a black comedy way. He was Dr Strangelove. Who was?

3 All in black, he rode into town in *Shane*. He got his deserts in the end. Name him.

4 He made a fine baddie as Rupert of Hentzau in the 1952 version of *The Prisoner of Zenda*. Who did?

5 Who was the wicked Sir Guy of Gisbourne to Errol Flynn's Robin Hood?

6 In *Dial M for Murder*, who hired the unsavoury Captain Lesgate (Anthony Dawson) to kill his wife?

7 An easy one. Who played Dracula in the Hammer film *The Horror of Dracula* (1958)?

8 Who was the Godfather?

9 A leading baddie in the 1930s, then a superstar, he played a vicious baddie again in *The Desperate Hours*, Frederic March being the goody! Name him.

10 Lee Van — is a notorious baddy in Spaghetti Westerns.

11 A really mean bullying baddy, but he was a nice shy guy in *Marty*. Name the actor.

12 Back in 1932 he came to life as the Mummy, after his famous Frankenstein's monster. Who did?

13 He may have been nice as the Doctor in the House, but he was horrid in *The Blue Lamp*. Who was?

14 Lovable in many films, but not as a wife-murderer in *Monsieur Verdoux*. Who is the actor?

15 You know you are in for a chilling time when fat Sydney — and little Peter — are in a film.

16 Gentle, smooth and chilling is the American actor, Vincent — ?

17 She was bad in *The Letter* and worse in *Whatever Happened to Baby Jane?* Who was?

Musical interlude

1 Who wrote a very popular piece called 'The Four Seasons'?

2 What connection has pop star Kate Bush with Emily Bronte?

3 His song, 'Werewolves of London', was a Spring hit in 1978. Name the singer.

4 The chart-topper was 'Denis', the group was — ?

5 Brahms wrote five symphonies. True or false?

6 Which of Beethoven's symphonies is known as the Pastoral?

7 Who wrote the music later used for the words of 'Land of Hope and Glory'?

8 He wrote symphonies, operas, folk songs and a much loved 'Fantasia on Greensleeves'. Who did?

9 What has pop star Gerry Rafferty got in common with Sherlock Holmes?

10 Which universally loved singer died in 1977 after playing a game of golf?

11 Who wrote a series of Brandenburg Concertos?

12 Fill in the blanks in these folk songs: 'Sweet Lass of — Hill'; '— in our Alley'; 'Cockles and —'.

13 Which famous conductor met Mickey Mouse in *Fantasia*?

14 Who wrote a War Requiem and a Spring Symphony?

15 Sir Malcolm Sargent was a famous pianist. True or false?

16 Which conductor is the outsider? Leonard Bernstein, Colin Davis, Sir Charles Groves

17 What does *andante* mean?

18 A fiddle is not the same as a violin. True or false?

19 How many 'families' of instruments are there in a symphony orchestra and what are they?

20 What instrument does Benny Goodman play?

21 Who wrote a 'Scottish' symphony?

Swashbuckling stars

Once upon a time they made straightforward and gripping adventure films for boys (and most girls) aged from eight to eighty. Alas, they no longer do, but most of the golden oldies turn up on TV. Here are some questions about some of them.

1 Errol Flynn was the Robin Hood, but who played Prince John?

2 Dashing Tyrone Power played the lead in *The Mark of* —.

3 Who starred in *The Crimson Pirate*, in which his acrobatic training came in handy?

4 Captain Blood made a star of Errol Flynn. The villain was to be his enemy on other occasions. Who was he?

5 In *Lives of a Bengal Lancer* the star was an American, but few complained. Who was he?

6 In which film was Errol Flynn an Indian?

7 In which film set in World War I was Basil Rathbone Flynn's commanding officer?

8 Who played the handsome hero of *Ivanhoe*?

9 Who played the handsome hero of *Quo Vadis*?

10 In *The Private Lives of Elizabeth and Essex*, Errol Flynn played the dashing Earl of Essex. Who played Elizabeth I?

11 Opposite is the heroine in *Quo Vadis*, *King Solomon's Mines* and *The Prisoner of Zenda*. Name her.

76

12 The great director, John Ford, made *Wee Willie Winkie*, a rousing story of British India. Who played the young heroine?

13 In *The Drum*, a young Indian actor played a prince. Who was he?

14 Most of the Errol Flynn film, *The Charge of the Light Brigade*, took place in India, not the Crimea, but no matter! Who was the heroine?

15 The 1939 *Beau Geste* was a winner. Ray Milland and Robert Preston played his brothers. Who played the hero?

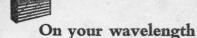

On your wavelength

1 Who invites you to 'Stop the Week' every Saturday on Radio 4?

2 When did direct broadcasts from the House of Commons begin?

3 Where is *The Archers* broadcast from?

4 Who plays Doris Archer?

5 What programme has followed the 9 am News on Radio 3 for many years?

6 Which 'Night is Music Night' on Radio 2 and has been for many years?

7 In 1978 the Glums were back on radio, resurrected from the famous old show *Take It From Here*. Can you name the entertaining cast?

8 Freddie Grisewood was chairman of *Any Questions?* for many years. Who is the present chairman?

9 On which channel can you listen to a story every morning?

10 Who presents *The Monday Movie Quiz* on Radio 2?

11 Who was the first General Manager, then Director General, of the BBC?

12 What was 2LO?

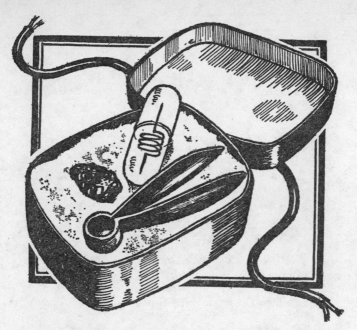

13 Pictured here is part of an early radio set. What was its nickname?

14 *Bandwagon* (1938) was the first real radio comedy with central characters and a story to be heard in Britain. It starred Arthur — and Richard —.

15 In 1978, a famous Yorkshire actor died who ran a popular quiz show called *Have A Go* for many years. Can you name him?

16 She was 'The Forces' Sweetheart' in World War II and a constant broadcaster. Name her.

17 Whose catchphrase was, 'the day war broke out'?

18 Whose catchphrase is – 'Aythangyew' (I thank you)?

Movie musicians and artists

Film-makers tend to 'improve' the lives of painters and musicians, so some of the films below cannot honestly be called factual . . .

1 *Rembrandt* was a magnificent film. Which big Yorkshireman played the great painter?

2 Who was the artist in *The Agony and the Ecstasy*?

3 Some say *A Song to Remember* is one to forget because of the script, but it was a huge success. Cornel Wilde was the actor; who was the composer?

4 Which artists did Kirk Douglas and Anthony Quinn play in *Lust For Life*?

5 In which Disney film did Karl Boehm play Beethoven?

6 His legs suitably hidden, Jose Ferrer played which dwarfish French artist in *Moulin Rouge*?

7 Dirk Bogarde looked very convincing at the piano playing which composer in *Song Without End*?

8 Not everybody approved of Ken Russell's *The Music Lovers* about Tchaikovsky. Who played him?

9 In *Night and Day* Cary Grant played which popular American composer?

10 Smooth George Sanders starred in a film of Somerset Maugham's *The Moon and Sixpence*, based on an artist who went to the South Seas. Who?

11 Stewart Granger played which legendary violinist in *The Magic Bow*?

12 Which artist's paintings were used in the Alec
    Guinness film, *The Horse's Mouth*?

13 Robert Morley played Gilbert in *The Story of Gilbert
    and Sullivan*. Who played Sullivan?

14 Kerwin Mathews played which composer in the
    Disney film, *The Waltz King*?

15 Before playing Jesus of Nazareth this actor played the
    title-role in *Mahler*.

16 Clifton Webb starred in *Stars and Stripes* about a
    composer of marches. Who was it?

SCENE I
TAKE I

Star gazing

Presenting some superstars of the silver screen! How many of these actors and actresses can you identify?

1   Can you recognise these three opera composers?

2   Fill in the blanks – *Tristan and —*, *The Pirates of —*,
    Orpheus in the —.

3   In which opera does a caddish American naval
    lieutenant desert his Japanese wife?

4   Handel did not write operas. True or false?

5   Which Gilbert and Sullivan favourite is set in the
    Tower of London?

6   What is a libretto?

7 In which opera does the heroine jump off the top of a Roman castle after it is discovered that she has killed the chief of police?

8 What nationality is Joan Sutherland?

9 Wales has an operatic knight. Can you name him?

10 When was opera 'invented': 1597, 1620 or 1700?

11 One of the most popular of all operas stars a gypsy girl who works in a cigarette factory. Who is she?

12 What happens at Glyndebourne?

13 Fill in the Gilbert and Sullivan blanks: *Trial by* —, *HMS* —, *Princess* —.

14 Who wrote the music of the pop opera, *Jesus Christ Superstar*?

15 The legend of a phantom ship inspired a German composer to write an opera. Name it and him.

16 The world's most famous opera house is in Milan. Do you know its name?

17 It has a famous grand march and is set in Ancient Egypt. Name the opera and the composer.

18 In which Gilbert and Sullivan work does 'the very model of a modern major-general' appear?

19 Can you name the singer who invented a name for herself based on her Australian birthplace?

20 Which is the higher voice, baritone or tenor?

Men at war

There have always been war films and there probably always will be. Some are just adventure films, others are sensational and a few are serious and reasonably truthful. Now for some questions . . .

1   Many regard *All Quiet on the Western Front* as one of the greatest war films. Which war is it about?

2   Over which river did prisoners build a bridge in a famous film starring Alec Guinness?

3   In *The Caine Mutiny*, who played the mentally unbalanced Captain Queeg?

4   In *The Desert Rats* which famous German general did James Mason play?

5   In *The Great Escape*, which American actor made an amazing getaway attempt on a motor bike?

6   In which film of a true story was a corpse 'planted' on the Germans, complete with false plans?

7   Who starred in *Sink the Bismarck*?

8   Name six male stars in *The Guns of Navarone* – if you can!

9   In which nasty film were vicious criminals assigned for a highly dangerous mission?

10 In which film did Alan Ladd become a British paratrooper?

11 *The Red Badge of Courage* was much cut by MGM, but its quality survived. John Huston directed it. Who starred in it?

12 In which film did a star dog go to war?

13 Which great British actor played Air Chief Marshal Sir Hugh Dowding in *The Battle of Britain*?

14 Which actress led many Chinese children to safety in *The Inn of the Sixth Happiness*?

15 There are newsreel films of the Boer War (1899–1902). True or false?

16 Who was the American forces' favourite pin-up in World War II? She is seen here showing her famous legs!

Curtain call

1 Which is the longest running play ever?

2 With which theatre do you associate Shakespeare and his colleagues?

3 Sir James Barrie wrote the most famous of all children's plays. What is it called?

4 The Royal Shakespeare Company's main home is at Stratford-upon-Avon. Where is its London home?

5 Who was the first actor to be made a lord for his services to the theatre?

6 Can you name these three Shakespearean characters?

7   When do you think gas lighting was first used in a London theatre: 1817, 1847 or 1867?

8   Do you know the name of the play on which the musical *My Fair Lady* was based?

9   Where are the flies in a theatre?

10 In which Shakespeare play does the hero say: 'To be, or not to be . . .'?

11 What was the name of the orange seller who first became an actress, then a favourite of Charles II?

12 What are the wings in a theatre?

13 What does a prompter do?

14 In which European country were the first great plays written and performed?

15 Who is Norway's greatest playwright?

16 Who is in charge of rehearsing a play?

17 Michael Croft runs a young people's theatre company. Can you name it?

18 Which of these shows was not written by Rodgers and Hammerstein? *The Sound of Music*, *Kiss Me Kate*, *South Pacific*

19 Tennessee Williams, Arthur Miller and John Osborne are Americans. Right or wrong?

20 Where might you see a Noh play?

The last picture show

1 He became a cult figure after his death because of *East of Eden*, *Rebel without a Cause* and *Giant*. Name him.

2 Who played Sir Thomas More in *A Man for All Seasons*?

3 How did the epic, *The Robe*, starring Richard Burton, make cinema history?

4 Who was Errol Flynn's leading lady in most of his best adventure films?

5 Who played *Paleface* and *Son of Paleface*?

6 Seen below is the most famous cross-eyed comedian of the silent screen. Can you name him?

7   Who starred in *The Man who Shot Liberty Valance*?

8   In which film did Charlie Chaplin mock Adolf Hitler?

9   Name the three Mills family stars.

10 *Barry Lyndon* is a long and beautiful film which some like and some do not. Who played the name part?

11 With which branch of the cinema do you associate Dimitri Tiomkin and John Williams?

12 Which director made *The Birds* in which our feathered friends attack humans?

13 Which film policeman was killed in *The Blue Lamp* but came back to life in a popular TV series?

14 In which film did Humphrey Bogart star with Katharine Hepburn and an old boat?

15 What full-length cartoon was based on a Beatles song?

16 In which film did Paul Newman perform clever tricks on a bicycle?

17 Who was the headmistress in the St Trinian's films?

18 Who do you connect with the phrase, 'You dirty rat!'

19 He was a 1950s superstar whose best known film was *The Great Caruso*. Can you name him?

20 Which crazy British team made a King Arthur film in 1975?

21 Was Deanna Durbin a dancer?

22 Who was out on a blustery day in a Disney film?

Answers

Page 8 Let's go to the movies

1 Judy Garland in *The Wizard of Oz*. 2 A lion (in the Disney cartoon film, *Robin Hood*, which dates from 1973. 3 The Keystone Kops. 4 'Spaghetti' Westerns made in Italy. 5 Gregory Peck. 6 His ears were too big. 7 Johnny Weissmuller. 8 Grace Kelly, now Princess Grace of Monaco. 9 Thrillers. 10 Nigel Bruce (left) and Basil Rathbone (right). 11 They are Abbott and Costello, the fat one being Costello. 12 *A Bridge Too Far*. 13 Sir Richard Attenborough was the director, Simon Ward the actor. 14 Sid James. 15 Fred Astaire. 16 He does not work the camera but arranges the lighting and is responsible for the atmosphere of each scene. 17 She has to note everything in a scene, so that the next scene in the same place with the same people will look exactly right. 18 101. 19 Shirley Temple. As Shirley Temple Black she became the American Ambassador to Ghana. 20 Los Angeles, California. 21 Roger Moore, who had played the Saint on TV, became James Bond in the later films. 22 Albert Finney.

Page 10 Ring up the curtain

1 True, though it is a man's role. 2 They are what the public calls footlights, and they are positioned at the front of the stage. 3 Aladdin's. 4 Molière (1622–73). 5 Stratford, Ontario. 6 The Old Vic Theatre. 7 You've hesitated or tripped up over a word. 8 Sir Ralph Richardson, Sir Alec Guinness and Sir Michael Redgrave. 9 Pitlochry. 10 Sir Terence Rattigan. 11 Cinderella. 12 In 1660 the first professional actresses appeared, boys having played women's parts earlier. 13 The Palladium. 14 In Britain a Rep or Repertory Theatre performs a new play each week, fortnight, three weeks or more, then goes on to the next play. Strictly, though, the word means a repertoire, or

group of plays, being given over a period, with a change of
play most nights. 15 Richard Burbage. 16 Regent's Park.
17 Oscar Wilde. 18 A free seat. 19 Acting that is too
overdone and crude. How it came to be called 'ham' is still
argued about. 20 The Abbey Theatre, Dublin.
21 Desdemona (in Shakespeare's play). 22 Henry Irving
in 1895.

Page 12 Television time

1 John Le Mesurier. 2 John Cleese. 3 Susan Hampshire.
4 Gerald Harper, who, apart from being a well-known
actor, is a disc jockey on London's Capital Radio. 5 The
director, who chooses exactly which scenes and shots we
see and rehearses the actors. 6 Patrick MacNee, who has
been in all the *Avengers* series. 7 *The Likely Lads* and
Whatever Happened to the Likely Lads? 8 John Thaw (left)
and Dennis Waterman. The series is *The Sweeney*. 9 The
regular service started on 22 August 1932, four programmes
a week being shown, but programmes had been broadcast
via a BBC transmitter on a daily basis from 30 September
1929. 10 Leonard Rossiter in *Rising Damp*.
11 *Emmerdale Farm*. 12 Tony Selby. 13 *Beryl's Lot*.
14 *Nationwide*. 15 Young nurses. 16 Morecambe and
Wise. 17 Richard Briers and Felicity Kendal. 18 Edward
Woodward. 19 Johnny Morris in *Animal Magic*. 20 John
Alderton and Pauline Collins. 21 Cricket and tennis.
22 *Hard Times*, starring Patrick Allen, Timothy West and
Alan Dobie. 23 Noah Berry.

Page 14 Strike up the music

1 A wandering poet-minstrel of the Middle Ages. 2 They
put a 'mute' in the bell of their instruments to muffle the
sound. 3 The great Russian composer, Sergei Prokofiev.
4 AБBA. 5 It was Maud who was urged to come into the
garden in so many Victorian drawing rooms! 6 Handel,
the German composer who settled down in Britain. 7 Loud.

8 A viola, which is slightly bigger than a violin. 9 Franz Liszt, widely regarded as one of the greatest pianists who ever lived. 10 The French composer, Claude Debussy. 11 From the clock-like ticking sound at the beginning of the second movement of the work. 12 False. Louis Armstrong played the trumpet, but Benny Goodman plays the clarinet, performing classical works as well as the jazz for which he is so famous. 13 Robert Schumann. His wife Clara was a famous pianist and both of them befriended the young Brahms. 14 The Russian composer, Rimsky-Korsakov. 15 Frederick the Great, King of Prussia, in the mid-eighteenth century. 16 Two violins, a viola and a cello. 17 Tchaikovsky, the most popular of all Russian composers. 18 Glenn Miller, Duke Ellington and Joe Loss. 19 *Israel in Egypt*, which is by Handel, the other two works being by J. S. Bach. 20 The violin.

Page 16 Screen scene

1 Laurence Harvey played the anti-hero created by John Braine in *Room at the Top* and also Colonel Travis in *The Alamo*. 2 He was a silent star who appeared in Westerns. 3 A non-speaking actor in films. 4 Peter Ustinov. 5 All of them have been played in films by Charlton Heston. 6 Dick van Dyke and Sally Ann Howes. 7 Terry-Thomas. 8 Australia. 9 Wyatt Earp. 10 Elizabeth I. 11 Michael Caine. 12 *The Man from Laramie*, which starred James Stewart. 13 *A Hard Day's Night*. 14 Grace Kelly. 15 Grace Kelly. 16 June Allyson. 17 Marilyn Monroe. 18 Laurence Olivier. 19 Anthony Quinn. 20 Clark Gable, who for some years was the leading male star of his day. 21 *Snow White and the Seven Dwarfs*. 22 From left to right: Harold Lloyd, W. C. Fields and George Formby.

Page 18 On with the dance

1 The choreographer, who is the most important person

because he creates the ballet. 2 Moscow. 3 Tchaikovsky.
4 Melba, who was an Australian singer. Nijinsky and
Pavlova were both famous Russian dancers. 5 Because the
foundations of ballet were laid in France in the seventeenth
century, hence ballet terms are nearly all in French. 6 A
dance for two. 7 At the Royal Opera House, Covent
Garden. 8 Early in the nineteenth century. 9 Dame
Margot Fonteyn. 10 *Così fan Tutte* as it is an opera,
the others being ballets. 11 Dame Alicia Markova.
12 Anna Pavlova. 13 A turn on the leg: the dancer spins
round on one foot. 14 Dame Marie Rambert in 1926.
15 The dancer's ability to leap in the air. 16 Five.
17 Though he was born in Russia, most of his long career
has been in the United States, where his name is
particularly linked with the New York City Ballet. 18 *A
Chorus Line*. 19 False. It reached Russia from France early
in the eighteenth century. 20 In the 1830s in France,
though the most famous one appeared in Offenbach's
Orpheus in the Underworld in Paris in 1858. 21 A ballerina
dances the main roles in the classical ballets, but
occasionally a dancer is so exceptionally brilliant that she
is given the supreme title named in the question, which
shows that she is the absolute mistress of her art. 22 He
trains dancers and takes rehearsals, unless the choreographer
is present, when the latter is in charge. 23 In 1957. 24 La
Scala, Milan.

Page 20 Spaghetti – and other dishes

1 *A Fistful of Dollars*, which made Clint Eastwood, of TV's
Rawhide, world famous. It appeared in 1964. 2 *For a Few
Dollars More* and *The Good, the Bad and the Ugly*. 3 *The
Sheriff of Fractured Jaw*. 4 Spain. 5 a *A Professional Gun*;
b *Once Upon a Time in the West*; c *Hang 'em High*;
d *Navajo Joe*; e *The Big Gundown*. 6 a *The Overlanders*;
b *Eureka Stockade*. 7 *The Magnificent Seven*. 8 South
Africa, on a diamond field.

Page 22 On the box

1 Petra. 2 Large. 3 Ernie Wise, according to Eric Morecambe. 4 *The Big Match*. 5 Meg Mortimer, played by Noele Gordon. 6 Lindsay Wagner. 7 Melvyn Bragg. 8 Leonard Nimoy's (Mr Spock). 9 David Janssen. 10 In Mike Yarwood's show, with Mike playing them all. 11 They both run 'chat' shows in which they interview celebrities. 12 Henry Winkler. 13 *Sesame Street*. 14 Bob Monkhouse. 15 Bamber Gascoigne. 16 Lee Majors. 17 Jack Hargreaves, Marian Davies, Fred Dineage and Jon Miller. 18 Batman's young friend is played by Burt Ward. 19 Jack Howarth. 20 *Mixed Blessings*. 21 The late Richard Dimbleby and his sons, David and Jonathan. 22 Tennis. 23 John Stride. 24 Donald Sinden, a versatile actor who plays modern comedy roles in between major Shakespearean and other classical performances in the theatre.

Page 24 All the world's a stage

1 *Antony and Cleopatra*, *Timon of Athens* and *Troilus and Cressida*. 2 Richard Sheridan (1751–1816). 3 *Oliver Twist* was brilliantly turned into *Oliver!* by Bart. 4 It was a rest room or club room for actors; the original one must have been decorated in green. The term dates back to the eighteenth century. 5 Three. 6 Henry V in Shakespeare's play. 7 *Oklahoma!* by Richard Rodgers and Oscar Hammerstein. 8 It is the actors' trade union. 9 True, and they wore different ones for comedy and for tragedy. 10 True. An actor named Booth shot him in a Washington theatre in 1865. 11 Christopher Marlowe. 12 Four, the first being built in 1663. 13 The Citizens'. 14 Anton Chekhov. 15 Broadway. 16 Shakespeare. 17 Eton. 18 Yul Brynner. 19 True. 20 When an actor forgets his lines. 21 Royal Academy of Dramatic Art.

Page 26 What's in a name?

1 *A Fistful of Dollars.* 2 *High Noon.* 3 *Paint Your Wagon.*
4 *The Slipper and the Rose.* 5 *The Sting.* 6 *Star Wars.*
7 *True Grit.* 8 *The Four Feathers.* 9 *Jaws.* 10 *Candleshoe.*
11 *Lady and the Tramp.* 12 *The Thirty-nine Steps.*

Page 28 Across the channels

1 Liverpool. 2 Gordon Jackson. 3 Alan Bates. 4 True,
though on the great day few people actually had television
sets. 5 Barry Evans. 6 Bill Oddie, Tim Brooke-Taylor
and Graeme Garden are the popular trio. 7 Arthur Lowe,
whose performance is regarded as a small screen classic.
8 Fletcher, more often referred to as 'Fletch'. The sequel
was *Going Straight.* 9 *Blue Peter.* 10 The City Varieties,
a beautiful small theatre in Leeds, Yorkshire. 11 Cannon
is the private eye – the private detective – of the trio, and
tubby with it! 12 Violet Carson. 13 No less a genius than
Rudolf Nureyev. 14 Lord Louis Mountbatten, the uncle
of Prince Philip and the Queen's cousin. 15 Nicola Pagett,
who had earlier been one of the stars of *Upstairs,
Downstairs.* 16 Reginald Bosanquet, who is a news reader
on ITV. (Angela Rippon, because she is a woman, is too
easy!) The others read the news for the BBC. 17 She
went down in the *Titanic.* The actress who played her was
Rachel Gurney. 18 Derek Jacobi. 19 Barry Foster.
21 Magnus Magnusson, who also does excellent
programmes on archaeology. 22 Pam Ayres.

Page 30 Cinema story

1 *The Godfather*, which was a tough, thrilling film about
crime and the Mafia. The others are all Westerns. 2 Judy
Garland. 3 Cary Grant. 4 King Kong was a giant ape, as
most readers must surely know, but the other animals
were dogs. 5 Olive Oyl. Yes, the spelling is right!
6 Pinocchio. 7 Warner Brothers. 8 The director. He

97

rehearses the actors and shapes the film, each shot being his choice. He – above all others – can turn a film into a work of art. 9 Left to right: Bob Hope, Jerry Lewis and Danny Kaye. 10 Charlie Chaplin, who became Sir Charles not long before he died. 11 Errol Flynn, whose Robin Hood is widely regarded as the best of them all. He also starred in *The Charge of the Light Brigade*. 12 Robert Shaw. 13 *Carry On Up the Congo*; it hasn't happened yet. If it has by the time this book comes out, we apologise! 14 Paul Newman and Robert Redford. 15 Sir Alec Guinness. 16 Rooster Cogburn, the tough, unscrupulous and hugely enjoyable lawman in *True Grit*. 17 Bing Crosby and Bob Hope did not make *The Road to Alaska*, but, happily, they took the other two roads. 18 Wrong. Stan Laurel was British and a Lancashire lad, like so many great comics. 19 Laurence Olivier, who also directed these three films. 20 Believe it or not, these are the actual names of Doris Day, John Wayne and Kirk Douglas in that order. 21 *Doctor No*, with the Doctor played by Joseph Wiseman, while Bond was, of course, Sean Connery. 22 Jodi Foster. 23 Walt Disney.

Page 32 News and views

1 John Craven. 2 Richard Baker. 3 Shaw Taylor. 4 Miriam Karlin. 5 Robert Powell. 6 'Duchess'. 7 *Clapperboard*. 8 Dave Allen. 9 Yootha Joyce. 10 Birmingham. The BBC has a major studio there. 11 Robert Hardy. 12 *Wings*. 13 Angela Rippon's. 14 HMS *Ark Royal*. 15 From left to right: Cannon – William Conrad; Rockford – James Garner; Barlow – Stratford Johns. 16 Alfred Burke. 17 John Logie Baird in London in 1925. 18 Patrick Cargill. 19 1967 for the public in Britain, but John Logie Baird transmitted colour back in 1928! 20 Terry Nation. 21 A horse race; the Derby was televised in 1931. 22 True.

Page 34 On wings of song

1 Maria Callas. 2 Scottish Opera. 3 Richard Wagner.
4 1946. 5 *The Merry Widow*. 6 Rossini wrote the *Barber
of Seville* and Mozart *The Marriage of Figaro*. 7 Brahms,
who wrote no operas. 8 Benjamin Britten. 9 1946.
10 Soprano. 11 Giacomo Puccini (1858–1924). 12 *The
Gondoliers*. 13 The conductor. 14 *Rigoletto* by Verdi.
15 Tito Gobbi is a great baritone, the others were famous
tenors. 16 The Bolshoi Theatre in Moscow. 17 *The Magic
Flute* (Mozart), *Boris Godunov* (Mussogksky), *Billy Budd*
(Britten). 18 *Hansel and Gretel* by Engelbert Humperdinck
(no relation!).

Page 36 Movie time

1 Jules Verne, the 'father' of science fiction. 2 This story
with a South African mining setting starred Roger Moore
and Susannah York. 3 Omar Sharif. 4 Mark Lester, who
held his own memorably in a very powerful cast.
5 Pollyanna, the heroine of Eleanor Porter's ever popular
novel. Hayley Mills played her. 6 James Stewart, who
played a small but memorable role in the classic film, as
the doctor who tells John Wayne . . . no, we mustn't spoil
the story for those who have not seen it. 7 Dinah
Sheridan. Her unfortunate husband was played by Scottish
actor Iain Cuthbertson. 8 No. Lee Van Cleef was the
leading character in this last of the series on the subject.
9 Flicka was a horse. The boy was Roddy McDowall.
10 *On Her Majesty's Secret Service*. 11 Sabu. He had
started life as a stable boy in India and was spotted by the
director Robert Flaherty. This led to his first memorable
performance in *Elephant Boy*. Though he made films as a
man – he died in 1963 – it is for his youthful performances
in films like *The Thief of Bagdad* that he is best
remembered. 12 *The Love Bug*. 13 Audie Murphy, whose
'baby' face disguised the fact that he was one of the
bravest men to serve in the American Army in World War

II. 14 Sean Connery and Michael Caine. The original
story was one of Kipling's. 15 Frank Morgan. 16 Paul
Newman, Robert Redford and numerous others. 17 Robert
Redford, the sympathetic lawman who had to go after the
unfortunate Indian on the run. 18 *The Slipper and the
Rose*. 19 Johann Strauss the younger, the composer of
'The Blue Danube' and other favourites. 20 *Tora! Tora!
Tora!*, a truthful big screen epic. 21 *They Died With
Their Boots On*.

Page 38 Keep in tune

1 Benjamin Britten. 2 Nine. 3 Percussion. 4 Handel's
Messiah. 5 'The Mull of Kintyre'. 6 Jimmy Young.
7 The usual form of a concerto is a work in which the solo
instrument or instruments (piano, violin etc.) play with an
orchestra and form a contrast to it. The work is often in
three movements. It can also mean a work without soloists,
which is explained by the fact that the word simply means
'concert' in Italian, or 'concerted music'. 8 It means
'plucked'. At a concert you may see the string players
plucking at their strings instead of using their bows to
produce the sound. 9 De Falla, because he was Spanish,
the rest were Italian. 10 Dvorak. Its full name is 'From
the New World'. The Czech composer wrote it in
America and parts of it show the influence of black folk
music. 11 Paganini (1782–1840). 12 Tchaikovsky's Sixth.
He approved of the sad title. 13 The Shadows. 14 St
Cecilia, her day being 22 November. 15 From left to
right: Purcell, Britten and Elgar. 16 Frederick Delius
(1862–1934). 17 Schubert. His Eighth Symphony has
only two completed movements. No one knows why it was
never finished. 18 Joseph Haydn, who visited Britain twice
in the 1790s. The music does not describe the two cities,
the names being suitable 'labels' to commemorate his work
in Britain. 19 Stephen Foster (1826–64), an American
who died very poor. 20 He invented the saxophone around

1840, and other instruments. 21 Sir Edward Elgar. 22 Jan Paderewski (1866–1941) was Prime Minister for a short time in 1919, but resigned. 23 The French composer, Hector Berlioz, the name being given the work because it describes strange events in an artist's life.

Page 40 Stage struck

1 John Gielgud. 2 Ralph Richardson. 3 Laurence Olivier. 4 The National Theatre. 5 A classical Greek theatre. 6 George Bernard Shaw. 7 Shakespeare's Globe Theatre.

Page 42 Mickey Mouse & Co.

1 The sorcerer's apprentice. 2 Vivien Leigh. 3 *Carry On Sergeant.* 4 Pinewood, because it is a British studio, the others are American. 5 Gene Wilder. 6 Three. 7 *Genevieve.* 8 Elvis Presley's. 9 The *Doctor* series: James Robertson Justice played the ferocious Spratt. 10 Burt Lancaster. 11 Tom and Jerry. 12 Danny Kaye. 13 Marlon Brando. 14 Three. 15 The Marx Brothers. 16 D-Day, June 6th, 1944, when the Allies invaded Europe in World War II. 17 Lauren Bacall. 18 *Peter Pan* (the name of a song in the film). 19 Tweety Pie. 20 1928. 21 The name given to the statuettes awarded at the annual Academy Awards presentations in Hollywood for distinguished work in the previous year's films. The first were given in 1928 and it is said that the name Oscar came about because, when a girl saw the first one that had been struck, she exclaimed: 'It reminds me of my uncle Oscar!' 21 Rex Harrison.

Page 44 Turn on the radio

1 Roy Plomley. 2 1922. 3 ITMA (It's That Man Again). 4 Robert Robinson. 5 Antiques. 6 Cricket. 7 David Jacobs. 8 Peter Sellers, Harry Secombe and Spike Milligan were the immortal trio. 9 1922 – it was a boxing match. 10 *Under Milk Wood* by Dylan Thomas. 11 Ed

Stewart. 12 *Waggoners' Walk*. 13 1951. 14 The arts.
15 Nicholas Parsons. 16 Alistair Cooke's. 17 Sid James
and Bill Kerr. 18 The BBC Symphony Orchestra. 19 Pete
Murray. 20 *Any Questions!* 21 David Allan and Wally
Whyton. 22 From left to right: Ed Stewart, John Peel
and Pete Murray.

Page 46 Keep on your toes

1 Prokofiev. 2 The dancers who are not soloists and are
the equivalent of a chorus. 3 Hungary. 4 Spain's.
5 American. 6 Sadler's Wells Theatre in London. 7 *Swan
Lake*. 8 The Bolshoi. 9 The Royal Danish Ballet.
10 Stravinsky. 11 Kenneth MacMillan's. 12 He was a
choreographer, his finest work being for Diaghilev's
Russian ballet early in this century. 13 Stuttgart.
14 Petrouchka. 15 Odette-Odile. Both parts are usually
played by the same dancer. 16 Spain. 17 Sir Frederick
Ashton and Sir Robert Helpmann. 18 Maurice Béjart.
19 Dowell. 20 Beryl Grey.

Page 48 More movies

1 Alec Guinness. 2 Audrey Hepburn. 3 Yes, including
The Magnificent Two. 4 Clint Eastwood, who also directed
the film of that name. 5 Stanley Baker, later Sir Stanley.
6 John Wayne. 7 Will Hay. 8 Faye Dunaway. 9 *Bullitt*.
10 How Mr and Mrs Adamson reared lion cubs in Kenya.
11 Mel Blanc. 12 Doris Day. 13 Charlie Chaplin.
14 Margaret Rutherford. 15 Tony Curtis. 16 *The Jazz
Singer* (1927). 17 Robert Newton. 18 Metro-Goldwyn-
Mayer. 19 Peter Finch for his fine performance in
Network. 20 Mary Pickford, a star of the silent era.
21 *Singing in the Rain*.

Page 50 TV who's who

1 Timothy West. 2 Private Pike. 3 *Are You Being
Served?* 4 Patrick Moore, the BBC's astronomer. 5 Terry

Scott and June Whitfield. 6 Ian McShane. 7 Richard
O'Sullivan. 8 France. 9 William Hartnell. 10 Lee
Remick. 11 Frank Windsor. 12 Joseph Cooper. 13 Jon
Pertwee. 14 1955. 15 Peter Falk as Columbo.
16 Geraldine McEwen. 17 Richard Beckinsale, in the
Ronnie Barker series, *Porridge*. 18 *The Good Old Days*.
19 Bonnie Langford. 20 They were all in *The Avengers*,
though at different times. 21 Glaze; *Crackerjack*. 22 Anna
Ford. 23 John Noakes, Peter Purves and Lesley Judd
presented *Blue Peter*. Lesley still does. 24 Sian Phillips
played Boudicca in *The Warrior Queen*.

Page 52 Film festival

1 *The Gold Rush*. 2 Greta Garbo. 3 Peter O'Toole.
4 *Patton*. 5 Natalie Wood. 6 Victor Mature and Hedy
Lamarr. 7 Boris Karloff. 8 John Mills. 9 A biographical
film. 10 *Apache*. 11 Elizabeth Taylor. 12 Dustin Hoffman.
13 Charlton Heston. 14 *The Sound of Music*. 15 *The
Cruel Sea*. 16 *North-west Frontier*. 17 David Niven and
Cantinflas. 18 The Fonda family.

Page 54 The play's the thing

1 St Joan, which is also the name of the play. 2 The
Mermaid. 3 John Laurie. 4 300. 5 An actor who goes on
stage as a replacement if the actor he is 'understudying' is
taken ill. It can be a nerve-wracking job! 6 A performance
in which an actor or comedian dresses up as a woman.
7 He is out of work! 8 Emlyn Williams. 9 1576, near
Finsbury Fields, which was then on the outskirts of north
London. 10 Rex Harrison – in New York and in London.
11 Acting without words, expressing feelings with the face
and the body. 12 Chichester. 13 It is the slope which
runs down from the back wall to the footlights. 14 She
looks after the costumes of the actors and actresses.
15 Noël Coward. 16 Holy Trinity Church in Stratford-

upon-Avon. 17 *Cinderella*. 18 False, he did *not* write a
Henry VII. 19 Iago. 20 Sir Michael Redgrave.
21 Bottom. 22 True. He made his name in *A Streetcar
Named Desire* on the New York stage.

Page 56 At the pictures

1 *Cat Ballou*. 2 Hayley Mills with John Mills. 3 Richard
Burton. 4 Michael Caine. 5 Lon Chaney. His son – Lon
Chaney Junior – was notable in the same field! 6 Leslie
Caron. 7 *Darby O'Gill and the Little People*. 8 Tarzan.
9 *Going My Way*. 10 Douglas Fairbanks. 11 Mia Farrow.
12 Joan Fontaine and Olivia de Havilland. 13 Stuart
Whitman. 14 James Fox. 15 *The Dam Busters*. 16 Barbra
Streisand. 17 Frank Sinatra. 18 They were singing
cowboys who starred in many 'singing' Westerns.

Page 58 Take the right steps

1 Degas. 2 *The Rite of Spring*, choreographed by Nijinsky
with music by Igor Stravinsky. 3 Dame Ninette de Valois.
4 *Spartacus*. 5 Marie Taglioni. 6 *The Nutcracker*. 7 Serge
Diaghilev, the sensation happening in Paris in 1909 and in
London not long afterwards. 8 Lynn Seymour. 9 Sir
Robert Helpmann, also a distinguished actor. 10 *Coppélia*.
11 Rudolf Nureyev. 12 Moira Shearer. 13 Nijinsky.
14 Norman Morrice. 15 *The Sleeping Beauty*. 16 *Prince
Igor* by Borodin. 17 *The Nutcracker*. 18 *Billy the Kid*.
19 Sir Frederick Ashton. 20 The springiness of the feet
of a dancer.

Page 60 In the picture

1 *Match of the Day*. 2 *It's a Knockout*. 3 *Crossroads*.
4 *World in Action*. 5 *Magpie*. 6 *Batman*. 7 *Crackerjack*.
8 *Blue Peter*. 9 *Coronation Street*. 10 *Angels*. 11 *The
Magic Roundabout*. 12 *Nationwide*.

Page 62 The magic of the movies

1 *Gone with the Wind.* 2 Judy Garland. 3 Joyce Grenfell.
4 Jean Harlow, a star of the 1930s. 5 From left to right:
Robert Morley, Ernest Borgnine and Wilfrid Hyde White.
6 Elizabeth Taylor. 7 *The Wild Bunch.* 8 Leslie Howard.
9 Jeffrey Hunter. 10 Richard Harris. 11 *The Railway
Children.* 12 Alan Ladd. 13 Bert Lahr. 14 Richard
Burton. 15 *Waterloo.* 16 Terence Stamp, in front of an
admiring Julie Christie. 17 Esther Williams, a very fine
swimmer who starred in many films in and out of the
water. 18 *Giant.*

Page 64 It's instrumental

1a French horn. b double bass. c bassoon. 2 Handel.
3 Ravel; he was French, the other two were English. 4 At
the Royal Albert Hall in London. 5 Woodwind. 6 Sir
Alexander Gibson. 7 False. He went deaf. 8 Beethoven.
9 Sibelius, the great Finnish composer. 10 André Previn
is a conductor and pianist, the other two play the guitar.
11 Forty-six or forty-seven. 12 Nashville, Tennessee.
13 Sextet. 14 Joseph Haydn. 15 False, though the vast
majority of his works were for the piano. 16 Folk music.
17 Figaro. 18 Mendelssohn. 19 The flute. 20 Six.
21 Engelbert Humperdinck 'stole' the name of the German
composer. 22 False: he is best known for his magnificent
military marches. 23 Doctor Thomas Arne (1710–78).

Page 66 What a carry on!

1a *Cleopatra.* b *Constable.* c *Up The Khyber.* d *Cabby.*
e *Follow that Camel.* f *Teacher.* g *Sergeant.* h *Screaming.*
2a Kenneth Williams. b Kenneth Connor. c Hattie
Jacques. d Sid James. e Charles Hawtrey. f Bernard
Bresslaw. g Peter Butterworth. h Joan Sims. i Jim Dale.
j Jack Douglas. 3a Gerald Thomas. b Peter Rogers.
c Talbot Rothwell.

Page 67 Time for heroes

1 David Niven. 2 Virginia McKenna. 3 Anna Neagle.
4 *In Which We Serve*, one of the finest films made about
World War II. 5 Errol Flynn.

Page 68 Turn on the telly

1 Eddie Waring. 2 Jimmy Hill. 3 Leif Erickson. 4 She
starred in the prison series, *Within These Walls*. 5 *Weekend
World*. 6 *The Muppets*. 7 Hilda Baker and Jimmy Jewell.
8 *Magpie*. 9 Donald Hewlett. 10 *The Hong Kong Beat*.
11 Emily Richard. 12 Programmes about archaeology and
history. 13 Racing. 14 Stewart Granger. 15 David
Attenborough, brother of Richard. 16 From left to right:
Benny Hill, Jimmy Tarbuck and Ronnie Corbett.
17 Christopher Timothy. 18 William Franklyn. 19 James
MacArthur. 20 Paul Eddington. 21 Eammon Andrews.
22 The family of Laura Ingalls Wilder, on whose delightful
and informative books the series is loosely based.

Page 70 Camera angles

1 *The World's Greatest Athlete*. 2 *The Wooden Horse*.
3 *Swallows and Amazons*. 4 *The Swiss Family Robinson*.
5 Donald Sutherland and Elliott Gould. 6 *Little Big Man*.
7 Nelson Eddy and Jeanette MacDonald. 8 Charles
Laughton. 9 *Thoroughly Modern Millie*. 10 Charlton
Heston. 11 *Bambi*. 12 Gregory Peck and Charlton Heston.
13 Jill Ireland. 14 Marty Feldman in *Sherlock Holmes'
Smarter Brother*. 15 *The Absent-minded Professor*.
16 Victor McLaglen. 17 *Johnny Concho*, which starred
Frank Sinatra.

Page 72 The baddies

1 Charles Laughton. 2 Peter Sellers. 3 Jack Palance.
4 James Mason. 5 Basil Rathbone. 6 Ray Milland,
playing the part of Tony Wendice. 7 Christopher Lee –

who else? 8 Marlon Brando. 9 Humphrey Bogart. 10 Lee
Van Cleef. 11 Ernest Borgnine. 12 Boris Karloff.
13 Dirk Bogarde. 14 Charlie Chaplin. 15 Sidney
Greenstreet and Peter Lorre. *The Maltese Falcon* was one
of their joint nasty efforts. 16 Vincent Price, the suave
villain in many a horror film – and a star in other sorts of
movie as well. 17 Bette Davis, a star for more than forty
years.

Page 74 Musical interlude

1 Vivaldi. 2 A song called *Wuthering Heights*, the name of
Emily Bronte's great novel. 3 Warren Zevon. 4 Blondie.
5 False, he wrote four. 6 His Sixth, which was inspired
by Beethoven's feelings about the countryside. 7 Sir
Edward Elgar. 8 Ralph Vaughan Williams. 9 He sings
'Baker Street' in which street Sherlock Holmes lived!
10 Bing Crosby. 11 Johann Sebastian Bach. 12 Richmond;
Sally; Mussels. 13 Leopold Stokowski. 14 Benjamin
Britten. 15 Though he played the piano, he was a famous
conductor. 16 Leonard Bernstein because he is American
and also a composer; the other two are British. 17 Not
slowly as some think, but at a moderate speed. 18 False:
it is. 19 Four: strings, woodwind, brass, percussion.
20 Clarinet. 21 Mendelssohn.

Page 76 Swashbuckling stars

1 Claude Rains, in *The Adventures of Robin Hood*. 2 *The
Mark of Zorro*. 3 Burt Lancaster. 4 Basil Rathbone.
5 Gary Cooper, and he was not the only American in the
cast, which included Franchot Tone and Richard
Cromwell. However, there were two British stalwarts on
parade, Sir C. Aubrey Smith, who had played cricket for
Sussex in his day, and Sir Guy Standing. The film was
made in 1935. 6 *Kim*. 7 *Dawn Patrol*. Rathbone had been
a Shakespearean actor before going to Hollywood.
8 Robert Taylor. 9 Robert Taylor. 10 Bette Davis.

11 Deborah Kerr, pronounced Karr! 12 Shirley Temple. In Kipling's story the name part is a he! 13 Sabu. 14 Olivia de Havilland. 15 Gary Cooper, who was forced back from the dead by Marty Feldman to appear in *The Last Remake of Beau Geste*.

Page 78 On your wavelength

1 Robert Robinson. 2 2 April 1978. 3 BBC Birmingham, as befits a programme about a Midlands farm. 4 Gwen Berryman. 5 *This Week's Composer*. 6 Friday. 7 Jimmy Edwards, June Whitfield and Dick Bentley as the gormless Ron. 8 David Jacobs. 9 Radio 4. 10 Ray Moore. 11 Sir John, later Lord, Reith. 12 The most famous forerunner of the BBC, into which it was amalgamated after some months of broadcasting in 1922. 13 A 'Cat's Whisker'. 14 Arthur Askey and Richard Murdoch. 15 Wilfrid Pickles. 16 Vera Lynn, who not only sang at home, but travelled to the war zones, including the grim Burma front. 17 Robb Wilton's. 18 Arthur Askey's.

Page 80 Movie musicians and artists

1 Charles Laughton, who was born in Scarborough. 2 Michelangelo, played by Charlton Heston. 3 Chopin. 4 Van Gogh and Gauguin. 5 *The Magnificent Rebel*. 6 Toulouse Lautrec. 7 Franz Liszt. 8 Richard Chamberlain. 9 Cole Porter. The name of the song may have given the answer to some readers. 10 Gauguin, who gave up being a successful stockbroker to become an artist and finally settled in Tahiti. 11 Paganini. 12 John Bratby's. 13 Maurice Evans, an English actor who settled in America but came back to make the film. 14 Johann Strauss junior, the most famous of the family of 'waltz kings'. 15 Robert Powell. 16 John Philip Sousa. In Britain the film was called *Marching Along*, but we have given its American title because it is more helpful!

Page 82 Star gazing

1 John Wayne. 2 Shirley Temple. 3 Buster Keaton.
4 Humphrey Bogart. 5 Judy Garland. 6 Alan Ladd.
7 Fred Astaire. 8 Paul Newman. 9 Johnny Weismuller.
10 Marilyn Monroe. 11 Stan Laurel. 12 Oliver Hardy.

Page 84 Night at the opera

1 From left to right: Verdi, Wagner and Mozart. 2 *Tristan
and Isolde* (Wagner); *The Pirates of Penzance* (Gilbert and
Sullivan); *Orpheus in the Underworld* (Offenbach).
3 *Madam Butterfly* by Puccini. 4 False: he wrote more
than forty. 5 *The Yeomen of the Guard*. 6 The words of
an opera. 7 *Tosca* (Puccini). 8 She is Australian. 9 Sir
Geraint Evans. 10 1597, by a group of poets, musicians
and scholars who hoped to recapture the spirit of the drama
of Ancient Greece. Instead, they invented a new art.
11 *Carmen* in Bizet's very popular opera. 12 An annual
opera festival in an opera house in Sussex. 13 *Trial By
Jury*, *HMS Pinafore*, *Princess Ida*. 14 Andrew Lloyd-
Webber. 15 *The Flying Dutchman* by Richard Wagner.
16 La Scala. 17 *Aida* by Giuseppe Verdi. 18 *The Pirates
of Penzance*. 19 Nellie Melba, born Helen Mitchell near
Melbourne, which city inspired her professional name.
20 Tenor.

Page 86 Men at war

1 World War I (1914–1918). 2 The River Kwai. The
story is fictional, as many survivors of the actual prison
camp at the river have hastened to point out. 3 Humphrey
Bogart, in one of his finest roles. Also to be recommended
to older readers of this quiz book is the original novel by
Herman Wouk. 4 Erwin Rommel, the famous commander
of the German 'Afrika Corps' in the Western Desert of
North Africa. James Mason also played the role – a
starring one – in *Rommel, Desert Fox*. 5 Steve McQueen.

6 *The Man Who Never Was*, which starred Clifton Webb and Robert Flemyng, also Stephen Boyd. **7** Kenneth More and some splendid ships, though some of them were models – and looked it! **8** Gregory Peck, David Niven, Stanley Baker, Anthony Quinn, Anthony Quayle, James Darren, also James Robertson Justice and Richard Harris. With an all-action story thrown in, no wonder it made a fortune! **9** *The Dirty Dozen*, starring Lee Marvin, Ernest Borgnine, Robert Ryan, Charles Bronson and other 'baddies'. **10** *The Red Beret*. And how did an American come to be in the British paratroopers? He was serving with the Canadians! **11** Audie Murphy. The film is a magnificent one set in the American Civil War and based on a great novel by Stephen Vincent Crane, who had never seen a shot fired in anger when he wrote it. **12** Lassie (who else?) went to war in *The Courage of Lassie*. **13** Laurence Olivier. **14** Ingrid Bergman played Gladys Aylward, the English servant girl who became a wonderful missionary in China and finally, a heroine. For those who want a more factual account with less romance, the real Gladys Aylward is described in the biography *The Small Woman*, by Alan Burgess. The film marked the last appearance of a much loved actor, Robert Donat. **15** True. **16** Betty Grable. Her films do not turn up on television as often as those of some stars of the 1940s, but she helped win the war in her way!

Page 88 Curtain call

1 *The Mousetrap*, which has already run more than a quarter of a century in London and is liable to run 'for ever'. In case anyone does not know, it was written by Agatha Christie. **2** The Globe Theatre, which was on London's South Bank, not far from where the National Theatre now stands. **3** *Peter Pan*. **4** The Aldwych Theatre. **5** Laurence Olivier, who had been a knight. **6** Left to right: Cleopatra, Falstaff, Othello. **7** 1817.

8 *Pygmalion*, by George Bernard Shaw. The musical keeps very closely to it. 9 Above the stage, where there are galleries from which scenery can be lowered or raised. 10 *Hamlet*. 11 Nell Gwynn. 12 The space to the left and right of what is called the acting area of the stage. 13 He helps out an actor who has had the misfortune to forget his lines by 'prompting' or reminding him of them. He (or she) hopefully gives the actor a few words loudly enough for him to hear, but (hopefully) not loudly enough for the audience to hear. It is not a pleasant job! 14 Ancient Greece, some 2500 years ago. 15 Henrik Ibsen (1828–1906). 16 The director, though up to a few years ago he was called the producer. 17 The National Youth Theatre. 18 *Kiss Me Kate*, which is based on Shakespeare's *The Taming of the Shrew*. Cole Porter wrote the very tuneful score and the show was later turned into a successful film starring Howard Keel and Kathryn Grayson. 19 Wrong. John Osborne is a British playwright, and the author of *Look Back in Anger* (1956), a play which greatly influenced the modern British theatre. 20 In Japan. It is a form of theatre that dates back to the fourteenth century.

Page 90   The last picture show
1 James Dean. 2 Paul Scofield. 3 It was the first film to be shot in the wide screen process called Cinemascope. 4 Olivia de Havilland. 5 Bob Hope. 6 Cross-eyed Ben Turpin. 7 James Stewart and John Wayne. 8 *The Great Dictator*, one of Charlie's talking pictures. 9 John, Juliet and Hayley Mills. 10 Ryan O'Neal. 11 Film music. 12 Alfred Hitchcock. 13 PC Dixon (Jack Warner). 14 *The African Queen*. 15 *Yellow Submarine*. 16 *Butch Cassidy and the Sundance Kid*. 17 Alastair Sim. 18 James Cagney. 19 Mario Lanza. 20 The stars of the TV programme *Monty Python's Flying Circus* – John Cleese, Graham Chapman, Terry Gilliam, Eric Idle and Michael Palin made *Monty Python and the Holy Grail*. 21 No, she was a singer in films of the 1930s and '40s, and a big star. 22 Winnie the Pooh in *Winnie the Pooh and the Blustery Day*.

More Beaver Books

We hope you have enjoyed this Beaver Book. Here are some of the other titles:

Enjoying Ballet A Beaver original. Jean Richardson's survey of the history of ballet and today's best-known companies, performances and stars, illustrated with black and white photographs and with a foreword by Anthony Dowell of The Royal Ballet

True Adventures of the Wild West A Beaver original. Eighteen stories of the wild west, from Custer's Last Stand to the Alamo and the short-lived venture of the Pony Express, told by Robin May and illustrated by Harry Bishop

Auto Quiz A Beaver original. For car fanatics of all ages, a book packed with all sorts of quizzes and puzzles about cars and their engines, designers and drivers, roads, rallies and racetracks. Written by Sandy and Serge Ransford and illustrated by Terry Dutton

Wild Jack Set in the twenty-third century, this exciting story for older readers tells of a young City boy's capture by Wild Jack, the notorious Savage, and the decision it forces him to make. Written by John Christopher, author of the highly acclaimed 'Tripods' books, also published in Beavers

New Beavers are published every month and if you would like the *Beaver Bulletin* – which gives all the details – please send a large stamped addressed envelope to:

Beaver Bulletin
The Hamlyn Group
Astronaut House
Feltham
Middlesex TW14 9AR

383237